HOW TO TUTOR and INFLUENCE PEOPLE

A Winning Approach to the World of Tutoring

ADAM MUCKLE

Copyright © 2024 by Adam Muckle
All rights reserved.

CONTENTS

Introduction 1

Some Famous Tutors to Inspire You 🖊 4

Some Films to Inspire You 🎥 6

Some Books to Inspire You 📚 7

Before They Were Famous 🖊 8

Permission 9

Why Tutor: Have A Clear Vision 11

Understand Why Parents Use Tutors 12

What to Tutor: Know Your Limitations 16

Language Matters 17

When and Where to Tutor 19

How Much to Tutor 21

How Much to Charge 22

Who to Tutor 24

Tutoring Materials 25

CASE STUDIES

Latin and Classical Greek 27

Scholarship Arts Subjects 29

11+/Pre-Test Preparation 30

Building Resilience in Students 33

Leadership and Mentoring 34

Building Confidence 36

Preparing for Sessions.. 38

Conduct and Ethics 39

Residential Tuition 42

Read, Read, Read…... 46

Self-Care and Self-Awareness.. 50

Conclusion 52

INTRODUCTION

Tutor. Student. One to One. You sit facing one another or next to one another. The potential to transform life-trajectory. Ready for launch.

I remember starting tutoring more than ten years ago. I remember being as nervous as ever embarking upon teaching my first student. How to fill the hour? What balance should I make in talking and explaining to letting my student deploy the skills he or she was learning? There didn't seem to be any particular guide open to me exclusively targeted at tutoring to prepare me.

Since that day, that first step on my journey, I have since taught hundreds of students in many different subjects. All my tutoring skills I have taken from my twenty years of school, university and law school experiences and tutoring practice. I have no formal teaching qualification. And yet parents internationally have sought me out to prepare their children for entrance exams, scholarships, public examinations or simply to learn a subject they haven't had a chance to at school. And my students have respectively achieved great success, reached their goals and even surpassed what they thought possible. It is a natural high to see my students do so well. Some have gone from beginner level to degree level as a result of my initial tutoring. It sparked an interest, a talent, a passion for a subject. It has been a joy to tutor and I feel like I haven't worked a day in my life. I am very lucky. I love what I do and found some sense of calling.

In contrast to my training to become a barrister in what seems a lifetime ago, for tutoring I made a point of meeting and talking to as many people 'in the know' as possible. I attended many tutoring events, organised several tutoring conferences, received professional tutoring awards and an honorary fellowship, judged tutoring awards and met many educators in that time. I am not so interested in apanthropy or its practitioners. You need to put yourself out there.

When I was President of The Tutors' Association for three years, building up the official professional membership body for all those involved in the tutoring sector in the UK, I wrote many articles about tutoring. I was almost at a point where I felt that I had exhausted all I had to say at the time on the matter. I had 'done my bit' in representing and giving back to a sector which had been very good to me. I have written about professional tuition, 11+ tuition, online tuition, scholarship tuition, language tuition, residential tuition… you name it, I've probably written a tuition article on it.

However, there was no single widely available book on the subject which a tutor - whether university student, graduate, teacher or someone considering an alternative career path - could just pick up and read. A book that explains what tuition is, where to tutor, when to tutor, why you should tutor, how to motivate your students to be the best, recommendations for effective tutoring; as many questions you may have that can be answered. I want this book to help you progress faster in tutoring than when I myself started. Explanations can make things less frightening and can give you the courage and confidence to do what you need to do. Whatever your background, you've picked up this book. This is for you. Happy tutoring.

SOME FAMOUS TUTORS
TO INSPIRE YOU

Socrates - Plato

Socrates was all about questioning, investigating and finding the truth. Plato was so inspired by his tutor he founded his own school in Athens, the Academy. Not to mention recounting many of Socrates' dialogues with his fellow Athenians.

Aristotle - Alexander the Great

A powerful teacher and philosopher following his tutor Plato, he became private tutor to no less than Alexander the Great at his father Phillip of Macedon's request.

Vernon Bogdanor - David Cameron

A British political scientist, historian and professor at Oxford and King's College London, he described his most famous student as one of the ablest he has taught.

Bertha Flowers - Maya Angelou

A mentor and example to Maya, Bertha taught her that literacy and intelligence are not synonymous, to value the gift of books and life, to trust her abilities and to find her own voice.

SOME FILMS TO INSPIRE YOU 🎥

Educating Rita (1983)

Seven Years in Tibet (1997)

The History Boys (2006)

Dead Poets Society (1989)

The Great Debaters (2007)

Good Will Hunting (1997)

Finding Forrester (2000)

Matilda (1996)

Coach Carter (2005)

The Karate Kid (1984)

SOME BOOKS TO INSPIRE YOU 📚

Jane Eyre by Charlotte Bronte

Goodbye, Mr Chips by James Hilton

To Sir, With Love by ER Braithwaite

Wonder by RJ Palacio

Anne of Green Gables by LM Montgomery

Lucky Jim by Kingsley Amis

Harry Potter and the Philosopher's Stone by JK Rowling

Percy Jackson and the Lightning Thief by Rick Riordan

Matilda by Roald Dahl

Boy by Roald Dahl

BEFORE THEY WERE FAMOUS

Barack Obama as a law professor insisted on class discussion; he didn't like to lecture. He used hypothetical, tough questions to develop and challenge arguments.

JK Rowling taught night classes in EFL (English as a Foreign Language) in Portugal while writing during the day. She was a single mum and training as a teacher while writing her first Harry Potter book.

These examples from public life, films and books show just what impact a tutor can make. You always remember the teachers and tutors who've made a real difference to the course of life. It is that simple and that profound. A child may come from a rich family or a poor family by happenstance of birth and parentage. The role of a tutor being *in loco parentis* is a privileged position to be in and be taken seriously. Your influence, your charm, your motivation, your inspirational words beyond the syllabus and exams can echo through eternity.

PERMISSION

Tutoring in the UK is at time of writing an unregulated sector. The opportunity to tutor is open to anyone. However, there are more expectations on a tutor now from society. There is a huge thirst for knowledge out there. Tutoring today is a multi-billion pound industry and has become more professional in the past twenty years. The sector was given government recognition with the establishment of The Tutors' Association in late 2013. I would highly recommend you join this professional body. It provides a lot of guidance, discounts and support for tutors, and opportunities to connect and collaborate with others in the sector. It will save you a lot of time in getting started. Unlike other tutoring community platforms in the industry landscape, its role is not-for-profit, constitutional, non-commercial and, importantly, democratic and representative of the entire sector, with regular elections for a board of directors every three years. It is thoroughly worth your support and time joining and getting involved. In addition, I found it a great way to serve, to give something back, alongside my tutoring work.

You will be expected to have at least a degree of qualification in the subject you profess to tutor. You will know your subject. You may not feel at times like you do know it but it is in there somewhere. You just have to dig it out of the back of your brain and drag it to the forefront of your mind again. *Docendo discimus.* ("Through teaching, we learn." Need a Latin tutor? Do not hesitate to get in contact!)

If you are expecting to tutor children or vulnerable adults the least you can do is to acquire an enhanced DBS certificate. Take what you are doing seriously. A couple of character references would be useful to prospective clients and other educators. Show that you are a reputable character if called upon.

WHY TUTOR: HAVE A CLEAR VISION

Alongside getting started up, think about how far you want to go with tutoring. Is this about tutoring an hour here or there to make a bit of money on the side or is it to be a real career move? Are you laying a brick or building a cathedral? Either way, think big to maximise your chances and have a clear vision of what you want to achieve. And believe that you can do it. See it. Believe it. Achieve it.

I recommend you become 'in the know' about what you are seeking to do. Make yourself an attractive prospect. You will find this is in you already if you are successful. Research tuition companies, news in the tuition sector, the technical language used in education, different schools of thought. Maybe you already have ideas that you can write about that can help you get your name out there and speed up the process of getting work for yourself. You are just bringing to the surface what has been unknown to others previously. Get out there.

But how do you get students to tutor?

UNDERSTAND WHY PARENTS USE TUTORS

Parents want your brain and your time. Parents themselves may or may not have the brains or the time to tutor their own children; maybe both! Their children may not want to listen to them trying to teach them something. It is a strain on the familial relationship and dynamics. This is so often the case as to why I have been called upon. It is not that the parents don't have capacity; it's whether their children will listen and/or whether parents have the time depending on the other areas of their lives. The chief reason is typically a high-demanding job, not that they don't want to spend time with their children. That's the sacrifice they are making and that is their choice. They call upon a tutor as a second voice, a more objective voice and ear, to come alongside their child and to guide them to a successful outcome, whatever that looks like academically. It is a triangular dynamic and you are part of that team.

Aspirations can be high. You are there to motivate to meet those aspirations but also to discern whether these are realistic. Eton may not be a realistic option; to have a range of schools, day and boarding, may be more appropriate. Is Timothy really going to get into the local grammar school with such low CAT scores? Is Tabatha really going to put Law at Cambridge on her UCAS application when she's being predicted straight C's? It is up to the parents whether they want to take on board your reality-check. Most parents I have worked with are open to what I have to say given my experience. However, you will no doubt encounter obstinacy and resistance at times.

As part of aspiration, parents may be interested in exploring their children's talents. Children may have shown interest in a particular subject not taught at school or a talent for something that someone has seen in them. For parents, it is worth exploring that and you are there to help them do that.

Knowledge gaps are another reason for finding a tutor and you are there to fill those gaps. Your student may have missed some classes for whatever reason or perhaps doesn't pay attention in class and has switched off. Your student may find actual learning of the material easier with someone there as a guide. You as a tutor have to hone in relatively quickly and sort the wheat from the chaff, focusing on training the weaknesses which will over time become strengths.

Parents don't always have time to support their children as they may have busy jobs which simply prevent them from spending as much time with them. They employ tutors to fill that time gap to keep their children's minds active and engaged, up to date with and sometimes beyond what is expected of the school curriculum.

Another big reason for parents to have a tutor, I believe, is to be a role model for their children. Someone perhaps who is closer in age to the children, bridging the generational gap to help both the children and parents to understand each other and their motivations. The child may be more likely to listen to you rather than their parents because you are seen to be outside of the family dynamic. The child can say what he or she wants without any apprehension or anxiety. They may think they are more likely to be listened to by you than their parents. And the parents recognise this and want to take a step back from this part of their child's education. They want someone who's been there and got the T-shirt and show a path for their children to follow.

For these reasons families can be very protective of their tutors. They won't let their friends know about your existence until the proof is in the pudding, until they see results. And that's fair enough. However, if your student has a younger sibling or siblings, trust that you will be the first the parents turn to for help. A real bond can be created with families and trust built over that time. There are potentially years more work for you with that family helping their children succeed.

Parents are looking for a role model for their child. They themselves can do that up to a point on a daily basis. However, when it comes to school work, there is clearly a limit to what parents can recall from their school days and a limit on the patience of the child to listen to his or her parents. That prospective life-long relationships can be tested to those limits.

You stepping into the family dynamic can prove a Godsend. Draw on your credentials and compare them with what the family is looking for to inspire their child. Be the inspiration to that child that may be more willing to listen to an outsider's advice rather than their parents'. Parents are grateful for your role in their child's academic and life progress.

As a result their child's confidence will grow as they see that someone trusts in their child's ability and potential. In my experience this is the principal benefit of tutoring and it is so rewarding to see a child achieve things they initially never thought possible.

WHAT TO TUTOR: KNOW YOUR LIMITATIONS

It is sensible and fair to cast your net wide when starting to tutor in order to gain experience. It gives you the chance to explore what you are really good at and narrow down a specialism and find your niche in a competitive marketplace. But know your limitations. Don't attempt to tutor Science if you're clearly an arts graduate; or attempt to tutor a five year-old if a parent asks you to, when you haven't even had any experience of managing that early years age group. Can you even remember being five? You may not have considered it, but it's harder to tutor younger children than older children. It takes a lot, a lot, of energy and patience.

LANGUAGE MATTERS

Be careful about the language you use to describe yourself as a tutor. The education sector can be fairly elitist about the word 'private'. When I was a boy being tutored in Classical Greek before the school day started, as it wasn't taught as part of the school curriculum, I thought private tuition just meant one-to-one. However, in society generally, at least it seems in the UK, it means money, unfairness, better resources, social mobility. The word 'professional' now is probably a more appropriate epithet as a catch-all term for tutors who work in tutoring as a living. It is a better mark of distinction compared to those who would be tutoring as a stop-gap while aiming at another career.

Aside from that, I could be described as an Arts Tutor, Scholarship Tutor, Classics Tutor, Common Entrance Tutor and a whole host of other labels. Choose the ones that reach and level with whichever audience you're trying to engage, and that will differ depending on the context. At the end of the day, you tutor.

The title or term 'super tutor' has been used by the media to describe industrial-scale tutoring, usually to describe those tutors who work with '(Ultra) High Net Worth' families at home or abroad. At the end of the day, whoever you are tutoring, from whatever background, you tutor.

I also try to use the word *sector* when discussing tutoring in the UK rather than *industry*, which implies profit and goes back to the debate about private education. The tutoring world has moved on from that. You as a tutor are an ambassador for tutoring, working as part of a body of educators. Be mindful of this.

WHEN AND WHERE TO TUTOR

So you're not a schoolteacher. Well you might be. More on that later. The point is your potential students are at school so realistically your tuition hours will be from late afternoon to late evening. Let's say 4pm to 8pm. You're in the service sector now; don't expect a typical 9 to 5. There's your student's extracurricular activities to be factored into timetabling a regular slot. Then there's logistics to consider. Where is your student based? Where are your other students based? Do you want to rush around house to house like a headless chicken at peak rush-hour traffic? That is what tutoring used to be like if you didn't tutor from home.

Fortunately the option of online tuition since the pandemic lockdowns is now commonplace and regularly accepted without persuasion by families. Technology is now ahead of the curve and there are more platforms to link tutors and students online. It also opens up timezones if you have the good fortune to extend your geographical reach through Europe, Africa, Asia and the Americas. Tutoring online internationally is possible in English as education is an example of British soft power.

Many families around the world are interested in coming to the UK to send their children to school. They are interested in the entrance exam preparation process as well as academic support throughout their schooling towards GCSE, A-level and IB to make sure their children are on the right track. You may even have the personal charm and good fortune to be invited to their home country during half-terms and summer holidays, it is a great opportunity to build more rapport with your students, their productivity and extend your cultural quotient along the way.

Homeschooling has also become more viable as an option to tutor. Given its rise since lockdowns during the pandemic, alternative provision has become more important given the increase in mental health and special educational needs. Some students may be homeschooled for a variety of reasons: SEN, bullying, transition to a new school, a new country, other family circumstances, elite sport etc. Although it isn't 'normal' for children to be removed from the school environment and miss part of their social development, there are reasons why this may become necessary at some stage or another in a person's life journey. This is to be accepted as you help your student through this time. From my experience, homeschooling has been a short-term option, with emphasis on a return to school in the near future. Equally, I know tutors who have supported children through homeschooling for a year or more. So it is an option worth exploring for tuition work, especially if you have a teaching qualification and are familiar with working through many subjects and following curricula.

HOW MUCH TO TUTOR

If you're serious about starting tuition you will want to get things moving. It may be a bit of a waiting game at the beginning after you start advertising your services. You'll want to get started with your first student as quickly as possible, build up your experience and then use that knowledge to feel confident in tutoring more students. You may want to tutor just two to three students a week, perhaps up to ten or twenty, for an hour per student. It depends how much each individual student demands of your time as well. It is simply up to you but I would advise you to keep things manageable. Don't be greedy in gathering students to glean the money. Learn to say no. Don't love the money. Love the tutoring; the rewards will soon follow.

You may already be a teacher and want an extra revenue stream on a private basis, away from the auspices of the school. Whether it be before the school day or at lunchtime or after school, or at weekends, be mindful. Your foremost work responsibility is the pupils you are teaching at the school. Everything, everyone else is extra. Avoid burnout and doing too much, regardless of how tempting it may be. One cannot serve two masters. If you want to do more tutoring, strongly consider moving to tutoring full-time. This is now a viable option. However, think how much impact you can make in one or the other and how you would like to be remembered. Everyone remembers their teachers, particularly the good ones.

HOW MUCH TO CHARGE

Investigate the market for tutoring, particularly your competition who are tutoring your subject areas. Go onto tutoring platforms and company websites. How much are they charging? How much experience do they have? How do you rate yourself against them? How much do you think you should charge against them to beat them to a client choosing you instead? What do you consider your worth? Trust your instinct. If nothing is happening as a result, reconsider what you are charging. Perhaps you have gone too high, perhaps too low to be considered in the first place. Know your worth. What are you willing to offer?

Don't just undercut. Go above and beyond what others are offering. Make this clear to your prospective clients. Another thing to consider is what sort of clients and students you want to attract. If you charge low you will get enquiries from families that may want tuition to top up what their children are learning at school; or university undergraduates wanting study support. However, if you are charging higher, you may attract enquiries from families who are seeking independent school entry and money is less of an issue, or a professional willing to invest their earnings to learning a new subject or language they didn't get a chance to at school. You will find a range of motivations to study and what people are willing to pay.

Take into account that there will be consultation with your client on the phone and by email to discover their needs and find out about their children. Are you going to factor this into your pricing? Will the client pay upfront or at the end of the month? I have always tried to keep things simple in terms of communication and invoicing. Mums (and dads) have busy lives and many commitments. Keeping things straightforward I find is best. Make them aware that all these things be taken into account. They may be paying for lessons per hour, but the extra things you're doing are being factored into that too. Don't sell yourself short.

WHO TO TUTOR

Having taken all the above into account, it is only now time to consider who to tutor and how to acquire students. Keep your net as wide as possible within your intellectual and geographical reach. By tutoring itself and testing your own limits, going beyond your comfort zone, you will then discover what is the best fit for you and where you find a sweet spot for your tutoring practice. So go big and specialise later.

Here are some practical ways you can garner your first students:

- Ads in the local newspaper
- Have a social media presence
- Join local education or tutor community groups, in-person or online
- Compare what others are doing and position yourself within that competition
- Blog and Vlog
- Google tuition platforms and companies
- Research tuition in the news, get the vibe
- Note the professional and commercial language used by practitioners
- Create your narrative and share your story

TUTORING MATERIALS

Just like a teacher at school, you will want to have the right materials to tutor effectively. You will want to find out the resources the school is using if applicable. You may be conducting the lessons as study support or for revision purposes towards a qualification. Your regular lessons could be supplementary and expansive rather than covering the same ground as the school. Either way you're going to need materials for both you and your student for the lesson.

In the internet age in which we live there are so many resources and websites that can help. There are countless Maths websites, a plethora of past papers from a variety of schools and examination boards and you also have your own background in what publications there are for your own specialist subject. Online communities can also tip you off about what texts are being used beyond the old-school classics. There is a freedom in tutoring to tailor these resources to the individual student's learning style. Some books will work at some points than others to teach a particular area or topic.

CASE STUDIES

LATIN AND CLASSICAL GREEK

I got into tutoring when I had just finished a Masters in Law and looking for something to do while making job applications. A friend from a Classics summer school ten years before, who coincidentally got into Law as well, suggested it to me. My eternal thanks to her! I haven't looked back.

Latin and Classical Greek are languages over two thousand years old. Being 'dead' languages this makes them relatively static in terms of curriculum development changes. I do not say this as a criticism. They are positives. The grammar and vocabulary can be mastered given the contact time with a student. As long as you and your student are in step with each component of verbs, nouns, conjugations and declensions and grammar constructions, it is more than doable.

It's also the sort of subject that students take on because they truly enjoy the language or at least the mental challenge. It has a logic to it, a paradigm like Maths and Music that makes sense with each building block encountered. The more you cover, the easier it should get.

There are of course a few bigger grammar hurdles to explain. This is more to do with English grammar comprehension rather than the look of the Latin. A student's English should improve profoundly alongside study of the classical languages. Through all the translation work your student will cover, the more history, philosophy, myth and civilisation topics he or she will be aware of. It is a study of humanity and understanding the world without even realising it at first.

Being such a bedrock of western education in schools through hundreds of years, there are a vast array of textbooks, primers, dictionaries and exercise books to choose to teach from. At school I learnt from the *Oxford Latin Course*: the epic saga of Quintus Horatius Flaccus (the poet Horace) with supporting cast Horatia, Scintilla, Flaccus and Argus. It has a strong grammar focus. The *Cambridge Latin Course* with its hero Caecilius (*est in horto*) seems to be more in vogue nowadays for beginners at schools. In my experience it has some interesting vocabulary choices and isn't as strong on grammar at the beginning. It is often a reason why I'm called upon to tutor: grammar issues are ironed out for the student to feel comfortable to move forward again with confidence.

Another modern course-book is *Latin to GCSE* by John Taylor and Harry Cullen. It has a very good grounding in unseen translation and exercises to consolidate the grammar it guides the student through. It is more 'wordy' than the Oxbridge courses mentioned above. However, each student will have their own learning style and preferences. It is more common than ever for me now to draw upon a variety of texts, including all of the above.

SCHOLARSHIP ARTS SUBJECTS

Preparing children for scholarship exams is mostly about motivating them to study, revise and effect writing skills necessary for structured, well-argued, appropriate responses that the school is looking for in candidates. Due to the level of quality of the papers, a candidate isn't necessarily expected to get 100% but they should be showing the potential that they could get the right answers if they did have the knowledge. The role of the tutor is to make the scholarship student as aware as possible of the world around them, the types of literature and material that could help them do this, and to buoy them through the scholarship preparation process.

So it is a blend of focusing on knowledge-heavy subjects such as Latin, French, History and Geography, Maths and Sciences, and learning writing skills to tackle any essay question or writing task that is presented. No mean feat for a 12 or 13 year old aiming for schools with prestigious histories. It can be a daunting process but you are there to help the child, and their parents, to make the process more bearable and to enjoy the learning journey.

11+/PRE-TEST PREPARATION

The challenge here for the student is, broadly speaking, in four areas: English, Maths, Verbal and Non-Verbal Reasoning. You've probably heard those rattled off numerous times over the years.

The reality for the tutor is that English and Verbal Reasoning can, in terms of getting your student to the appropriate level, be two birds killed with one stone. The rumours that boys are generally weak in English, in my experience, rings true. In most instances, I am there to motivate a boy to read and broadly improve his vocabulary. I recommend books which are both stimulating and challenging to read and I present vocabulary lists for independent study. Then you must survey the types of questions a student could face, the topics to cover, strengthen spelling, punctuation and grammar. Reading as much as possible helps with these and creates good lifelong habits. More on this later.

For Maths it is important for you to cover all the core, baseline areas so that whatever the student comes across in the paper, those areas will come into play. Times Tables, square numbers, triangles, angles, quadrilaterals, polygons, fractions and percentages. Making your student strong in numeracy will pay huge dividends for them in the exam. Once these areas are tight, then one can approach the practice papers, and the real thing, with confidence.

In my experience, Non-Verbal Reasoning is difficult to tutor. It really is about the cognitive ability of your student, and this one cannot teach. You can go over as many papers and identify as many varieties of questions, but ultimately it is up to them to develop that ability and become familiar with the material. Fortunately my students enjoy the challenge and see it more as a puzzle than study or work.

Another area of this entrance exam process is the interview after the exams are passed. For independent schools this is a big part of the process, perhaps holding as much weight as the exam itself, given the competition for places.

The school want to know about your student and how he or she can contribute to life at the school. Your student (*circa* 11 years old, remember) will probably never have faced a formal interview. So it will be necessary for them to explore for themselves who they are, their identity, their interests.

There is a psychological preparation to this. Ask your student to think about their interests, what the top things are in their life, what they are good at, what they regard as their achievements. These could be big or small. What matters to them.

Once these are at the forefront of their mind, you can explore a range of open questions to dig deeper into their interests, hobbies, subjects, family life, holidays, current affairs, prospective school etc, to help them to express themselves.

This is not about learning answers by rote or parrot-fashion. That is completely pointless and counterproductive for all parties. It is about getting children to converse confidently and comfortably about things they may not have considered before, with an adult who isn't their parent or teacher about themselves before the actual interview.

BUILDING RESILIENCE IN STUDENTS

A big part of your role as a tutor is to build confidence in your students and for them to believe in themselves. You are being engaged by parents to make their child realise they can achieve things they wouldn't initially think possible. On that journey, however, there may be significant challenges. There will be highs and lows, peaks and troughs. You and your student may have to overcome challenges and setbacks along the way. Your student may have to conquer a more significant adversary than a difficult Maths problem question. It may be a special medically-defined learning difficulty or a physical disability which may affect their self-esteem. How do you keep your student buoyant in these times? How do you help them develop the lifelong skill of resilience that will go way beyond the time you are tutoring them?

LEADERSHIP AND MENTORING

There are various sets of challenges for each successive leader. They require similar skills and qualities in order to face them. In our own lives and work we can be leaders. Parents, teachers and tutors are leaders in nurturing young people for them to find their own attributes and activities in life.

Based on my experiences, both as a tutor and President of UK tutoring's professional body, here are some attributes worth exploring for your tutoring practice:

- Create and pursue a vision, share that vision and instil belief
- Have passion for what you do
- Find allies, build your team and learn to trust
- Be a good listener
- Communicate with your team and advocate to others, both internal and external stakeholders
- Be prepared for a lot of conversations
- Seek out role models
- Seek out opportunities
- Seek knowledge
- Learn to manage people and expectations
- Learn from mistakes
- Grow emotional intelligence and self-awareness

- Grow awareness of different constituencies, other people's perspectives
- Take responsibility and be accountable
- Be decisive. Don't be afraid to take risks
- Be willing to make sacrifices, typically personal ones
- Lead by example but delegate where necessary
- Stay strong, stay resilient and never give up!

BUILDING CONFIDENCE

If you feel completely daunted by the prospect of becoming a leader, do not be afraid to ask for help. There are great resources, books and motivational speeches readily accessible to support you in your ventures. I found the following books incredibly helpful during my professional tenure:

- *Legacy - 15 Lessons in Leadership* by James Kerr
- *Leading by Sir Alex Ferguson* with Michael Moritz
- *Black Box Thinking* by Matthew Syed
- *Start with Why* by Simon Sinek
- *The Seven Habits of Highly Effective People* by Stephen R. Covey
- *Turn the Ship Around!* by L. David Marquet

Leaders make leaders. When it then comes to nurturing children's independence and exploring their own goals, whether through parenting, teaching, tutoring or mentoring, identify role models in their lives. In addition, getting children to think outside the box, to try a new sport or activity, bouncing ideas off them, is a gateway to new knowledge and new experiences. The recent books *You are Awesome* and *Dare to be You* by Matthew Syed are a great way for children themselves to do this. Autobiographies by public figures are also good: *Mud, Sweat and Tears* by Bear Grylls and *Becoming* by Michelle Obama being just two examples. There are many more out there to spur students to success.

PREPARING FOR SESSIONS

This is malleable depending on experience in your tutoring journey. However, when starting tutoring, preparation is key. Be ready with what you plan to cover in the session. Practise some elements of the lesson beforehand, on your own or with friends and family. You have to perform and impress your student with your knowledge that they want you to share.

As the hours of sessions increase over time you will become more familiar with the material you are tutoring and hopefully preparation won't seem as much of a chore. You will know what needs done and prepare quicker. And over time, you may feel like you're going on auto-pilot. However, be as professional and serious about your session as in your very first tutorial. Remember that first session and hold onto how much it meant, to you and your student.

CONDUCT AND ETHICS

How does a tutor operate in a professional manner? If you have not been trained for a professional qualification or worked in a professional role before, here are some practical pointers to consider:

- Integrity - Do what you say you're going to do, be straight with people, don't compromise. How you treat people matters and reveals everything about you. Integrity is everything. Let this be your personal creed.
- Safeguarding is of paramount importance when tutoring young people and vulnerable adults. You're creating an environment for your student to feel safe and comfortable with the freedom to ask questions, converse and with a focus on their individual requirements.
- Punctuality - be there and be square. We've all been there. The Zoom call on meetings waiting for enough people to just show up before the organiser to start. Waiting an age for someone you've agreed a particular time to meet in person. It's frustrating isn't it? And yes, life can get in the way sometimes, but you must endeavour to be there on time for your clients and students. Don't keep others waiting for you. It speaks

volumes. Perhaps it is that some people just aren't wired to be punctual. But for yourself and your tutoring work, it is crucial. Check your diary schedule, check the trains, check TFL. Time is precious. In commercial law, the expression 'Time is of the essence of the contract' is a central tenet. Turn up as if your lesson is starting fifteen to thirty minutes earlier if you've got a problem. No excuses.

- Presentation - do you know how to dress yourself? Turn up meaning business.
- Preparation - have your materials and stationery ready and demand that from your student too to be on an equal footing. Stay up to date with any relevant developments in education and technology.
- Devices - if they need to be used during the session, use them for that purpose. If they don't, don't take them out and distract yourself. That goes for both you as a tutor and your student.
- Communication - show clarity in presenting material and be able to explain your points appropriately. Use language your student can understand and which is relevant to the material.
- Rapport - build rapport with your student to establish an effective tutoring relationship, being professional and having parameters for that. You don't want to

create an unhealthy dependence. Know your own boundaries. It's a fine line between tutor and friend. You're there to teach first and foremost. Mentor not Best Friend. There is a difference. You want to foster independence, not dependence, on tutoring. There will come a time to move on, exams will be finished, tuition will end with that student and you will be ready for the next one.

When I was President of The Tutors' Association, some of the other Directors and I invited some of our members, more established in their businesses, to convene and discuss what should be included in tutoring guidelines beyond the Code of Conduct specifically. Eventually we managed to summarise these in a six page document. That may seem modest but you'd be surprised how long it took to be approved! It is important for professional organisations to have such documents as a matter of credibility and accountability. The document was very brief compared to other more established professional bodies. No doubt these can be finessed and added to, and these are there for the membership and tutors generally to read and take on board

RESIDENTIAL TUITION

This will really put you to the test. This will not just be about your skill as a tutor. It will be about how you conduct yourself as you become more involved in a family's world and their personal ecosystem. Tutoring is a subtle mix and balance of academia, business and society. Nowhere is this more in tune than when you are staying with a family over a short or long period. This is the time to demonstrate your charm, your charisma, your manners, your credentials to their fullest. You are now in the inner sanctum and part of the family furniture.

I have tutored all over Europe and Asia in the past ten or so years, for bank holiday weekends, half-terms, tuition over Christmas holidays, intense scholarship tutoring over Easter periods and the summer breaks. My first in Shanghai was the game-changer for me, tutoring a boy needing help with Latin and Greek for his Eton scholarship preparation, and his older brother wanting an introductory crash course in Law. Work begets work and I was asked to do similar tuition in Hong Kong the following year. Then it was Venice, Italy; Verbier, Switzerland; Normandy, France; KL, Malaysia; Singapore; Beijing and then a longer spell in India. I've also carried out regular tuition for families in Jersey, the Channel

Islands, Scotland and the Home Counties, all staying with or at accommodation close to the families.

Globalisation is very real. The families I have helped are typically ones that send their children to UK boarding schools, who are then home for the holidays, or they have dual heritage and identity. 'Home' is two places through their parents. There is no language barrier as my students all speak English, though their parents may not be as fluent. One student I tutored I discovered had set up the whole tuition placement on behalf of his mother!

You may well have your own accommodation which the family has booked for you. So there will be some level of separation and your own space. However, you will be there to serve the family, especially their child. You will be at their whim, their beck and call. Signed a tuition contract with the family? Well, there will be a few diversions from that along the way. There will be changes of lesson schedules as you fit in with family arrangements. There can be much waiting around. You may only be tutoring two hours a day or it could be a full day. You may not be tutoring at all on a day that you expected, at a moment's notice.

However, there is a lot of freedom with such a placement too. It is a great way to travel and see the world, increase your cultural quotient and to become much more outward-looking and build soft skills to a greater degree than hourly tuition. So you will be broadening your horizons in more ways than one. You will find that the more time you have to spend with your student the more you understand his or her personality and way of learning much better and help develop an open mind.

The client will typically organise all transport and accommodation arrangements, as well as settling all meals and bills. You may have the odd payment here and there but generally you should be well looked after. I spent five pounds sterling during my six months stint in Hyderabad, India.

You are there to tutor and the client will make sure you're comfortable and recognise the sacrifice of time you are making to be with their child. At its best, I have been chauffeur-driven to lessons in KL, Malaysia. I have even been given money to have a night out while the family had a function to attend in Patong, Thailand, but that's another story. Good times.

It is often useful to have a contact at home or a middle-person, someone who has your back, to relate any particular issues which may arise during the placement. He or she may not be able to help directly but the importance of venting a bit of frustration cannot be underestimated. A problem shared is a problem halved. It can make life a lot easier.

There will be some free time during these placements. Sometimes there will be more free time than tuition itself. Make the most of these times. You will have been paid to travel. It's a great opportunity to get some culture and see the world. The media will have you believe such tuition is commonplace, but they are rarer than you might think. Don't take such opportunities for granted. *Carpe diem*. Seize the day.

READ, READ, READ...

Whether a student is having tuition or not, I recommend all children always have a book on the go and read as widely as possible. More often than not I end a lesson asking my student what they're reading. This is to check whether they are reading but also to make recommendations based on their interests or to stretch them to read more challenging books for their development.

From my experience of tutoring, the best preparation for children to develop their minds is to read regularly. Whether it be fiction, biographies, history, encyclopaedias or keeping aware of current affairs through *The Week Junior* or *The Week* magazines, empowering children to be inquisitive is an investment in their future. Listening to the radio and watching TED and TED-ED talks and other fun and engaging educational channels on YouTube. Parents are understandably anxious about their children's use of technology. It is also a matter of familiarity with it. So it is worth exploring these channels and then allot time for their children to watch them, as appropriate. You as a tutor could be the key to recommendations!

There are various standard school reading lists readily available. Clearly some children don't like reading, so find short books for a reluctant reader, articles in newspapers and magazines, things they are interested in and enjoy, yet somewhat challenging at times. This will fuel their vocabulary and curiosity, their writing, their conversation and make them more rounded individuals, ready for interviews at the school. In all this, discuss with your child how things are going. Have open-ended conversations about the material they are reading and that they are confident, enthusiastic and resilient throughout.

Getting the most suitable books that each individual child would actually like to read can be difficult. Finding a series of books from one author that a child enjoys is a great way to foster a reading habit. You may consider getting *"The Reading Bug"* by Paul Jennings, which gives practical advice to help children love books. I would recommend a child reads thirty minutes a day or ten pages as a good target as a starting point.

Here are a selection of books I often recommend for 9 to 13 year olds, as well as some for young adults:

Mud, Sweat and Tears by Bear Grylls
Notes from a Small Island by Bill Bryson
A Short History of Nearly Everything by Bill Bryson
Millions by Frank Cottrell Boyce
A Monster Calls by Patrick Ness
The Lie Tree by Frances Hardinge
Holes by Louis Sachar

Rusty series by Ruskin Bond
The Ice Monster by David Walliams
The Boy at the Back of the Class by Onjali Q Rauf
Animal Farm by George Orwell
Nineteen Eighty Four by George Orwell
The Hate U Give by Angie Thomas
Catch 22 by Joseph Heller
Fahrenheit 451 by Ray Bradbury
His Dark Materials trilogy by Phillip Pullman
The Count of Monte Cristo by Alexandre Dumas
Long Way Down by Jason Reynolds
You are Awesome by Matthew Syed
Dare to be You by Matthew Syed
Wonder by RJ Pallacio

For more seasoned, mature and more scholarly students, perhaps stretch them with these suggestions:

The Undercover Economist by Tim Harford
Freakonomics: A Rogue Economist Explores The Hidden Side of Everything by Steven D. Levitt and Stephen J. Dubner
Prisoners of Geography: Ten Maps that Explain Everything About the World by Tim Marshall
Sapiens: A Brief History of Humankind by Yuval Noah Harari

Fermat's Last Theorem by Simon Singh
A History of the World in 100 Objects by Neil MacGregor
Alex's Adventures in Numberland by Alex Bellos
The Little Book of Thunks: 260 Questions to Make Your Brain go Ouch! by Ian Gilbert
Do You Think You're Clever? The Oxford and Cambridge Questions by John Farndon
I am Malala by Malala Yousafzai
The Greatest by Matthew Syed
The New Silk Roads by Peter Frankopan
To Kill a Mockingbird by Harper Lee
Fifty Things You Need To Know About History by Hugh Williams

SELF-CARE AND SELF-AWARENESS

While there is a lot of attention and focus on your students, and rightly so, it is as important to be self-aware and be mindful of your own mental well-being. You yourself have to be motivated to motivate and inspire your students. It is all very well to speak about never giving up, being relentless and persevere to fulfil goals, but you yourself have to have the will and energy to do so.

Tutoring can at times be very busy meeting demands of students, different curricula and their individual needs. Equally, conversations with parents about the role of tuition and their wishes can also be challenging. Make sure you get the right work/life balance and take appropriate time-out if necessary. Keep up your motivation and stay strong physically and mentally. *Anima sana in corpore sano.* A healthy mind in a healthy body. Eat well. Sleep well. Be well.

There are so many resources, podcasts and tools to keep you motivated. Use them to your advantage. Talk to others in tutoring or family members about any concerns you may have. A burden shared is a burden halved.

There can be a good deal of unintentional psychological pressure on a tutor. This can come from parents, students and other education stakeholders in a child's future prospects.

Remember that you are not Mary Poppins and you do not have all the answers. You are not superhuman. You are human, like everyone else, and there's only so much you can do yourself.

In order to equip you better, stay connected with other tutors, keep up to date with tuition practice by seeking out professional development opportunities such as educational courses and qualifications. These can all help you on your professional journey and keep you and your tutoring practice strong.

CONCLUSION

If you've reached this point having read through all these pointers, congratulations. Even if you've just skipped through to the end, you may wish to return to beyond the introduction. Just by the very act of picking up this book you're clearly serious about tutoring, or simply transmitting and communicating knowledge or a passion to a fellow human being. I've tried to answer in a straightforward manner the big questions to save you a lot of time in getting started tutoring. In a similar way, keep things simple for your students. They often just need someone to explain things clearly for them that they haven't had before, or they want to make quick progress through a subject towards a desired goal.

The tutoring process can be incredibly effective to accelerate a child's learning and personal development. You will sense if or when your tutoring is working. I have found that most of the time it does work but there will be occasions when it doesn't. You have to be honest with your parent client if it is not and explore other options for their child's best interests. There are plenty of children out there to tutor. You may be a minor or major cog in their educational journey and the education system as a whole. However significant your role, it is very powerful to see children achieve things they didn't think possible. And if it's working they will appreciate your role, both when you're tutoring and well into their futures.

Printed in Great Britain
by Amazon